# BEDTIME STORIES FOR STRESSED OUT ADULTS

Bedtime Stories For Stressed Out Adults: Eliminate Stress, Fear And Panic With Meditation Stories For Adults. Relax And Return To Dreaming

WALT PIXAR

© **Copyright 2021 - All rights reserved.**

The content contained within this book may not be reproduced, duplicated or transmitted without direct written permission from the author or the publisher.

Under no circumstances will any blame or legal responsibility be held against the publisher, or author, for any damages, reparation, or monetary loss due to the information contained within this book. Either directly or indirectly.

**Legal Notice:**

This book is copyright protected. This book is only for personal use. You cannot amend, distribute, sell, use, quote or paraphrase any part, or the content within this book, without the consent of the author or publisher.

**Disclaimer Notice:**

Please note the information contained within this document is for educational and entertainment purposes only. All effort has been executed to present accurate, up to date, and reliable, complete information. No warranties of any kind are declared or implied. Readers acknowledge that the author is not engaging in the rendering of legal, financial, medical or professional advice. The content within this book has been derived from various sources. Please consult a licensed professional before attempting any techniques outlined in this book.

By reading this document, the reader agrees that under no circumstances is the author responsible for any losses, direct or indirect, which are incurred as a result of the use of information contained within this document, including, but not limited to, errors, omissions, or inaccuracies.

# Table of Contents

INTRODUCTION ............................................................................. 7
CHAPTER 1: ACHIEVING HARMONY WITH YOURSELF ...................... 9
    What is Harmony? ................................................................. 10
    Developing Harmony with Yourself: Step by Step .................... 11
CHAPTER 2: ACCEPTING THE STORY OF CHANGE ............................ 20
    Change and Anxiety .............................................................. 22
    The Problem with Change .................................................... 24
    How to Accept Change ......................................................... 25
CHAPTER 3: LIFESTYLE THERAPY: LOOKING AT HYGGE AND OTHER WAYS OF BEING ................................................................................ 32
    What is a Lifestyle? ............................................................... 33
    Hygge ................................................................................... 35
    Yoga Lifestyle ....................................................................... 37
CHAPTER 4: DELETING DAILY STRESS: PREPARING FOR RELAXATION .. 42
    The Relaxing Environment .................................................... 44
    Preparing for Relaxation ....................................................... 48
    Relaxation Breathing ............................................................ 49
CHAPTER 5: BEDTIME STORIES: MINDFUL IMAGINATION ................ 53
CHAPTER 6: COLOR CONCENTRATION ............................................. 59
CHAPTER 7: SOUNDING SURPRISE .................................................. 69
CHAPTER 8: SMELL-O-VISION .......................................................... 79
CHAPTER 9: TASTING TREATS .......................................................... 89
CHAPTER 10: TOUCHING TEXTURES ................................................ 99
CONCLUSION ................................................................................ 108

# INTRODUCTION

Stress is not a sacrifice that should be made. You need to avoid it. Just as you need air to breathe and water to drink, you need to keep your mind free.

And yet, all too often, it can become incredibly difficult to fall asleep at night. Stress of what needs to be done can roil around in the mind.

You need to do everything that you can to help your body and your mind to let go of those worries and that tension, and sometimes, the best way to do so is through meditation and mindfulness.

This book is here to guide you through everything that you need in order to keep your mind free. It will teach you all of the mental habits that you need to begin to let go of those daily stressors and anxieties.

It will help you develop the ability and the mindset to release that tension and begin to unwind, and it does through, firstly through instruction on the habits that you need to know, but more importantly, through the use of bedtime stories.

## CHAPTER 1: ACHIEVING HARMONY WITH YOURSELF

Now, it is time to take a look at another method that you can commonly use to help yourself; achieving harmony. Remember, your body and mind are one. At the end of the day, you are you—there is nothing more than that. You are exactly who you are supposed to be; no more, no less. You have the strength that you need to be able to acknowledge that. You have the power that you will need to keep yourself fighting off that stress. You can help yourself become in tune with yourself, with your heart, and with your very mind itself. You can help yourself come together as one. Your body and mind, along with your soul, if you believe in it, are all connected. They are supposed to be balanced; this is a state in which you are able to pay attention to them equally. You are able to keep yourself balanced and centered. You are able to perfectly balance yourself.

All too many people focus on just one part of their being. Some are very firmly rooted in their bodies; they focus entirely on the way that they feel when they are sitting up or moving. They may recognize when the slightest changes have occurred in their bodies, recognizing when there is a shift in the way that they feel or behave. They can tell when something does not seem quite right for them physically, and yet, they are incredibly unaware of their mental states. Other people have the exact opposite problem; they focus entirely on their minds while losing sight of the world around them. They may live life in their daydreams, entirely avoiding taking a closer look at the ways in which they are able to interact. They do not look at the fact that, at the end of the day, they need to be paying better attention to what they see around them. They simply get lost in their thoughts and their emotions, not realizing the effect that doing so has on the body.

**What is Harmony?**

It is important to find a balance between body and mind; it is important to find that balance, that peace that exists within us when we are able to combine our bodies and minds, recognizing the importance of respecting them both, separately, but equally at the same time. They are both incredibly important. They both serve crucial roles that will keep you functioning, but at the end of the day, those roles that they serve can vary greatly. They can each create drastically different methods of the way that you live. They can show you very different tendencies and ways of looking at life around you.

When you can bring them together into one, however, you can help yourself. You become the best version of yourself, simply because you are taking the time that you will need to develop that greater understanding of who you are and what you do. By making sure that you are able to focus entirely on the way that you function, and making sure that you are entertaining that perfect balance, you achieve harmony within yourself. You achieve that ability to create a you that is perfectly you. You become precisely what you are meant to be, all because you are able to align that body and mind.


This is a bit of a long process. It can take time for you to figure out how to find that point of harmony. It can be a struggle for you to figure out precisely how you should be acting if you want to achieve that same degree of harmony. It does not have to be such a great mystery; you can learn to take those steps to achieve that best version of you. You can achieve that sensation of fulfillment and satisfaction. You can achieve that inner peace that comes from recognizing that, at the end of the day, you are doing precisely what you are meant to do.

**Developing Harmony with Yourself: Step by Step**
Remind yourself, before you begin to understand these steps to finding that inner harmony, that it is a long process. It is a journey that will take time and effort to get through. It is a

journey that is going to take your body and mind and find that common ground. It is going to find that inner place within you that will help you to become the greatest you that is possible.

Remember that you must be patient. Do not try to rush this; in rushing, you will be doing the exact opposite of what matters the most during this time. You must make sure that, at the end of the day, you are working with yourself, not against yourself. This means that you must make sure that you are focusing on yourself, your inner mind and peace, and how you wish to interact with not just yourself, but with the body. You must make sure that you are ready for the journey and the struggles that may come with it. You must ensure that, at the end of the day, you are focusing on becoming exactly what you need to be.

To get started, remind yourself that you are in this for self-improvement, not because you are punishing yourself for not being good enough. It is important for you to look at this as something that you want to do. You need to release that stress and that fear and then begin to embrace that personal harmony for yourself.

Let's take the time to go through the steps that you will need, the steps that will take you from point to point throughout the process to help yourself. These points are necessary to remember if you hope to ensure that at the end of day, you *can* succeed.

**Defining yourself now**

Begin by stopping and taking a deep breath. Think about everything that you are for a moment. Think of all of your achievements and who you are. Think of the strengths and the weaknesses that you have. What are you good at? What are you familiar with? Where do you struggle in life? What is it that you are right now, in this very moment?

To really discover that harmony within yourself, you must be able to recognize where you are now, as well as where you will be later. You will need to take the time to help yourself, to recognize who you are now so you can then begin to understand later where you would like to be. When you focus on this, you begin to see who you can be later on.

Take the time today, either right now as you are reading, or later before you go to sleep for the night, to really contemplate yourself. You need to create this mental image of who you are today. This is not the you that you wish to be;

it should be a perfect snapshot of the individual that you are as you sit there with this book.

## Defining who you wish to be

Next, you must recognize the person that you wish to be at the end of this all. What is your current goal? Who would you like to become? What would you like to be capable of later on? How can you achieve that? What can you do that will help you with that process, if not now, then at some other time in the future? This is the portrait of the you that you want to become; it is like your goals. Set that goal and then work toward it.

## Accept yourself

You must, to achieve harmony, totally and entirely accept yourself—the good, and the bad. You are not always going to like the actions that you go through. You will not always like the places that you end up in life. However, being able to recognize that you accept yourself and who you are is essential. Even when you make mistakes, own up to them. Recognize that you have made them and move on.

## Listen to yourself

Make sure that you also take the time to listen to yourself— you must be able to hear both your body and your mind as they work together to teach you. They will both constantly be working to communicate with you; they will have a lot of information to give, but you can only receive it when you are willing to listen.

## Meditation

To listen to yourself, you must meditate. Meditation will quiet your conscious mind; it will show you how you can soften the background noise and hear what really matters to you. It will help you to understand yourself better than ever before, so long as you are willing and able to concentrate entirely on the meditation itself. Meditation will be the focus at the end of this section; when you get to Part IV, you will see all of the information that you will need to get started with your own meditations, as well as how you can make them work for you.

## Respect your needs

In achieving that state of harmony, you must be willing to recognize what it is in life that you really want; you must be able to stop and remember what it is that matters to you and how you can achieve it. Pay attention to the ways in which you move, the ways that you interact with yourself and your mind, and more. You must be willing and able to see what you need, and more importantly, provide it for yourself.

## Gratefulness

As you continue working toward your harmony, you will find many times in which you may not have been as grateful as you should have been. Perhaps you did not thank someone for what they did, or take the time that you need to appreciate the truth of the matter when you have a relationship with someone. No matter what or why, we often forget, in such a busy world and in such stressful times, to be truly grateful to those around us. You must remember that, at the end of the day, you must ensure that you are grateful. You must remember that you need to be more willing to look on the bright side—gratefulness on its own is really just another form of positive thinking; if you can master it, you will find that, at the end of the day, you can succeed. You can thrive. You can find room to grow. All you have to do is embrace it all.

## Make it happen

As another point to finding that inner harmony, you must be willing to go for it. All good things need effort to make them happen and that means that you need to set out to work on your own mindfulness and meditations. You need to go out and be willing to facilitate the development of that harmony that you are looking for. It is only when you are willing and able to recognize that you get what you put in that you will be able to truly succeed.

So, do not wait another moment. Do not let another day pass by. Simply go out and embrace the changes that you are looking for. Remind yourself that you can in fact, become the you that you want to be. You can become able to adopt that harmony within yourself.

**Take responsibility**

You must also be willing to take on the full responsibility for yourself and your behaviors. Remember to recognize that you are the only one that is in control of yourself. You are the only one that matters at the end of the day in terms of what you can do and how you can do it. You can develop that ability for yourself, that capability that you need to recognize that you did something; it was not someone else's fault that things played out the way that they did. It is always your own, and the sooner you recognize that, the better.

**Take time to yourself**

Remember that, at the end of the day, you must ensure that you take time for yourself. You must make sure that you are quiet and involved with yourself sometimes. Allow yourself to focus on yourself, to enjoy yourself, and to quietly check in with yourself, body and mind. You must do this with love and acceptance, recognizing that you are precisely who you are, and accepting that as okay for you.

**Keep facing forward**

Above all else, you need to remember that you need to keep looking forward. While it is okay to glance over your shoulder from time to time as you walk, you cannot properly navigate if all you do is continue to look back behind you. You cannot properly get through the world if all you do is work backwards. You need to face forward, to focus on what comes next without dwelling or getting stuck in the past. When you can release that, recognizing that at the end of the day, you must make sure that you are able to move forward, you will make the progress that you are looking for.

# CHAPTER 2: ACCEPTING THE STORY OF CHANGE

Change is a normal part of life, and yet, it can be so incredibly overwhelming for us. People do not like change; they naturally resist it. They attempt to avoid it at each and every turn in life, and yet, despite that, it is still always there. We must practice acceptance, but at the same time change is like the complete opposite of that principle. Change is not acceptance at all—it is change. It is something shifting form what it was to what it will become. It can be scary for some people; if you do not know what your future holds, it could be terrifying. Even if you do know what comes next, it can be scary. It can be a major source of stress for so many people, who suddenly find that they are trapped, being moved around throughout space and time as if they cannot properly control it. They are tossed endlessly, from place to place, from time to time, and from event to event.

Change is not always within our control. It is not something that we can stop when it is something that is not directly related to or triggered by ourselves. You cannot stop change if it is something that someone eels does. Even then, there are types of change that you cannot prevent with yourself, too. Whether you like it or not, age changes you. The simple passage of time, year by year, month by month, week by week, and even day by day, can change us drastically. Think about it; one day, you are doing just fine. You are in a very normal situation for yourself. You have a good job, good friends, and a good relationship.

The next day? You get the news that you are about to be a parent unexpectedly. That is a major source of change; everything becomes different as soon as you have children, and there is nothing that you can do to resist that. From that point on, you are now a parent, and that brings with it all sorts of stressors, changes, and more that you will have to make. That brings changes to your schedules, to your priorities, and to your goals as well. That change may be the most welcome news in the world, but at the same time, the suddenness of it, paired with the finality of becoming a parent, entering that new stage in life, can be overwhelming.

You must be able to recognize that change, while unexpected sometimes, and while scary sometimes, and even while unpleasant sometimes, is a very normal part of life. It is normal for things to change. It is normal for life to go on, with or without you, and as surely as the seasons pass around you, and as surely as the leaves go from green to orange to brown before they fall, change will happen.

Your job, then, is to accept it. It is to recognize it. It is to remind yourself that, at the end of the day, you must be willing to accept and embrace that change for yourself. If you can do that, you can succeed.

**Change and Anxiety**

Of course, it is easy to talk about change as something that is simply there and that it should simply be accepted without any resistance. However, change is something that can cause a lot of anxiety. Remember, one of the reasons for feeling that anxiety in the first place is that you are afraid of what is going to happen. You may be terrified of what the world has in store for you, or worried that, despite your best attempts, you cannot deal with it. You might feel like coping with that change is next to impossible, or that you are going to be stuck, worse off than before, and that scares you. No matter the reason for your stress, and no matter how much that stress becomes something for you to fear, you must remember something: Change will happen.

If change gives you anxiety, you are not alone. Even good change can be overwhelming for many different people. It is easy to feel like change is weighing on you, or that it may even be expected sometimes. Think about it—when you have been together with your long-term partner for a socially acceptable period of time, everyone starts asking you when you are going to think about getting married. As soon as you tie the knot, everyone starts asking when the children are going to come along too. People are constantly pushing for more, more, more, and always trying to continue along with the changes.

Change is anxiety inducing, but at the same time, change signifies growth. It signifies being able to change the way that you look at the world, for becoming something new. It is something that is beautiful amidst the struggles and the discord. It is the rainbow after the storm, where you finally see what you have been working for. There are some growing pains somewhere along the way, but when you learn to see that, at the end of the day, the change that you encourage will bring with it beauty unlike that which you have seen before, you can begin to move closer to it. You can begin to see where you need to accept change and why it is something that we all resist.

**The Problem with Change**

Change is difficult. Change is something that people do not want to embrace because it is to go into something that I inherently different. Think about how many brides and grooms get cold feet right before walking down the aisle. Think about how many people have to tell them that things will be okay and that change is something to embrace, not something to fear? How often do mothers start to panic during their pregnancies, or even in their labors, claiming that they do not know what they were thinking and that they do not want to do this? How many people get a new job and then tell themselves that they need to do it without freaking out about it? Without worrying about the implications or the changes that follow along with it? You need to remember that, at the end of the day, change is scary, and usually, it is scary for one simple reason:

It is unfamiliar.

We, as people, are largely creatures of habit. We like routines; we like to go to sleep and wake up in the morning at the same time. We like to know what to expect. We like to have plans when we go out to do something. While there are exceptions to this rule and while some people thrive on the unpredictability of life itself, others thrive on that sense of normalcy; they need that normal life to feel like they know what they are doing. They need that sense of understanding what to expect, and because sometimes, when change is imminent, we feel like we are stuck, standing on the cusp of everything, tipping dangerously closer and closer to the edge of the unknown abyss in front of us, we resist. We dig in our heels. We fight the change because we want to keep that sense of normalcy; we do not want to see the world around us change into something we cannot predict.

**How to Accept Change**

For other people, however, change is not that source of anxiety. It is not that feeling that everything is going wrong. It is not that idea that, no matter how hard they try, they will continue to struggle. They embrace the change that they can see on the horizon. Like a surfer, learning to ride the waves instead of being scared and fighting them, you, too can learn to glide on the water. You can learn to hold onto that change. You can learn that you can, at the end of the day, continue to float along in the water without the stressors of life. You can learn to do this with ease; all you have to do is recognize that, at the end of the day, you need to accept change.

Yes, this means that you need to be able to recognize that change is imminent. You need to be wiling and ready to recognize that it is what you are looking for. It is that idea that you must be willing and able to stop and see that change does not need to scare you or make you feel like you are out of control; rather, you should be willing to flow with it.

Accepting change is something that is rather simple in theory—but in practice, it can be a challenge for those that find that they are the most resistant. You need to be willing and able to accept the change for what it is: Just that— change. You need to remove that power of fear from yourself. You need to let go of that terror that you feel at the idea of change. It may be unknown, but that is not necessarily a bad thing. When you can learn to accept change and you can learn to step away from the fear that change brings with it, you will find that you have already eliminated some of the biggest problems that you are struggling with.

The easiest way that you can help alleviate that fear of the unknown is to simply embrace the unknown. Think about it; people that go out into nature do not know what to expect that day. They may have general ideas about what they are doing or how they can expect to see things change around them, but at the end of the day, they are unsure what nature has to give them, and that is some of the excitement. Rather than being afraid of the change, try embracing it. See what kinds of new and exciting adventures that the universe brings along with it. They may be bad, sure—but they are just as likely to be grand.

Along those same lines, you must remember to keep your mindset positive when you are looking in the face of change. When it is just beyond the horizon, you need to remember this; you need to remind yourself that, at the end of the day, what you really need more than anything else is to remain positive, remain confident, and keep a cool head. Let go of that negativity; remember, if you label change as being bad or scary, you immediately gave it that power. You assigned that value to it, and without your intervention, it is simply change. There is nothing to it beyond that—it is only scary because you have labeled it as scary. You could have just as easily and readily labeled that feeling that caused your hear tot race in your chest as something else; it could be, for example, excitement at the change that is coming your way. It could have been a sensation of anticipation, of enjoyment, or of anything else, and yet, you have assigned the value of that fear to it. Instead of feeling afraid of the change in front of you, you must stop and think about things differently. You must stop and consider the fact that, at the end of the day, you need to do something more—you need to shift that thinking of yours into something more positive.

Finally, to complete the steps, you must make sure that you simply accept the change. You must simply do it—remember, so much of this book is about just biting the bullet and getting on with it. You need to—you cannot hope to create the change that you are looking for if you cannot get it from yourself. You need to make it happen and to do so, you must be willing and able to take that plunge. Take a deep breath. Face your fear head on. Look at it straight in the face. Tell yourself that it is not scary and that you are unafraid. Take the plunge and go.

But, you may say, maybe you *are* afraid. Maybe you and your family are currently coping with a sudden terminal diagnosis of a loved one, or are faced with trying to recover after a natural disaster, or after job loss, divorce, or even death. It can be harder to accept that change. You may feel like you are hurting, and rightfully so; it is normal to be hurting within those circumstances, and yet, you must also remember this point as well: You cannot simply paralyze your life because something unfavorable happened.

You are hurting. You are grieving. You do not want to move on because to move on is to accept the truth, and you may want nothing to do with the truth at this point in time. It could be that the truth hurts—perhaps a loved one has died. However, you cannot put a pause on that, no matter how hard you try, and no matter how rough it gets.

When you do face the truth, however, you can move on. You can begin to heal. You can embrace that, ultimately, life *has* been completely and utterly changed. You can recognize that, ultimately, life *will* move on, with or without you. If you are hurting, grieve your loss. Grieve for the change that you must face. And then, you must move on. Life will carry on, with or without you.

Finally, try to remind yourself of something important—it may be that, in the future, you will look back and remember that you are in a much better place at that point than you would have otherwise been. Perhaps you lost a job—but in going out for interviews, you met your soul mate. Life will take you for a spin, one way or another, and the best way to find somewhere safe and soft to rest is through making sure that, at the end of the day, you embrace the change. Let the change take you to where you are meant to be, and to where you will thrive.

# CHAPTER 3: LIFESTYLE THERAPY: LOOKING AT HYGGE AND OTHER WAYS OF BEING

We have spent quite some time now discussing the ways that thoughts, feelings, and behaviors come together full-swing. However, all of that can really be summarized up into one word: Lifestyles. The lifestyle that you choose to follow determines what you do, how you do it, and why you do it. It determines how you choose to behave, why you do what you do, and how you can, at the end of the day, ensure that you choose to live a life with the lifestyle that you are looking for.

When you change your lifestyle, so much more changes as well. You see changes in the way that you act. Your thinking shifts to embrace that new lifestyle. You spend allowing for those new lifestyles that you have chosen to shape everything about how you choose to live. If you choose to live a lifestyle that you know is going to be conducive to living a good life, you will find that you get all sorts of benefits provided to you. You will learn how you can live by those principles of that way of life that you admire. You can get the resources that you need to facilitate that new way of living. To shift the way in which you live to something more positive is something that you can do with ease and in doing so, you can better defeat stress in your life. You can learn to embrace these new ways of handling life around you in hopes of learning some very important principles from them.

We are going to take a look at two different philosophies surrounding how to approach stress. Each of these work slightly differently and produce slightly different results, and yet each offers their own benefits that you will need to admire and accept. You will need to look at the fact that the way in which you live your life will greatly change the way that you are able to look at the world. You will see through the eyes of the Danish—with their principle of hygge. You will also be introduced to the yoga lifestyle, taking a closer look at the principles that drive it.

Of course, this is not an exhaustive list. There are many other ways that you can live. There are all sorts of different lifestyles that you can embrace and choose to follow. You can learn to recognize the ways in which you are better able to live. You may choose to follow one of the lifestyles that you read about, or you may even find ways that you can sort of blend these principles together, creating something that is uniquely you and perfect for the lifestyle that you are hoping to embrace.

**What is a Lifestyle?**
A lifestyle is, at its simplest, a way of life. It is the way that everything that you do from what you think to how you make

decisions and everything in between, and how it all comes together. We typically think of lifestyles in the sense of being healthy or unhealthy, but the truth of the matter is that they can be so much more. Some lifestyles are incredibly soothing. Others focus heavily on mindfulness. Others still focus on bringing joy. We see these fly through social media rapidly, seeing trends such as the rejection of any items that do not spark joy within us, or in seeing this move toward yoga. However, that does not necessarily discredit any of those. Lifestyles have their own principles. They each have their own values, morally and fundamentally. They all focus on different aspects of what it means to be alive and how that can be managed and mitigated. When you are able to recognize the ways in which you can change your own lives, you can better deal with the world around you. You can better make choices when you have that list of principles and defining factors, all lined up nicely for you to see in front of you. It is so much easier to be able to look at the fact that you can make these changes to yourself when you know what you are aiming for—having a lifestyle that you have chosen to follow is perhaps the closest thing to an instruction manual as you are going to get when it comes to yourself, or own personal wellbeing, and everything surrounding it. When you are better able to take control of yourself, your mind, and everything surrounding it, you will find that success is not as difficult to manage. You will find that you can do better simply because you know better.

## Hygge

Hygge is a Dutch word that does not have a very clear way of being translated to English. It is a feeling that you get—it is the word to describe that comfort of curling up on your sofa with your favorite sweat pants on, wrapped up in your cozy blanket, listening to the drum of the rain on your window one dreary afternoon. It is that feeling of being able to slowly and contentedly enjoy the moment, comfortable and at ease with just the simple things.

Hygge is not about trying to live up to a name. It is not about trying to outclass someone or to be better than what those around you are. Instead, it is about learning to be comfortable and content with the little things—it is finding the joy in your mug of warm peppermint tea as you watch the snow drifting down from the sky. It is the way of life that the Danes swear by—it is a driving factor to them; a need to be cozy and happy that they strive to succeed.

Remember, Denmark, despite the intense winters that they have, is typically among the happiest countries in the world— and they attribute it to their hygge attitude. They bask in the simple contentment of just letting the moment hang in the air; they enjoy the nostalgia that can be brought on by your favorite comfort foods that remind you of your childhood.

Hygge does not have to be cold—it can happen in the summer, too; you could find a quiet enjoyment as you lounge in your yard, watching your children play happily in their little kiddie pool as you sip at your iced tea. It could be having a bonfire on the beach with your friends, contentedly, and perhaps not so quietly, enjoying each other's mere presence.

When you wish to live a hygge life, you are simply looking for that same degree of contentment. You are trying to live life while appreciating the simple things around you. You are learning to recognize that the way in which you live your life is powerful. You are recognizing that being able to accept the world, embrace it, and bask in the comfort of that acceptance is perhaps the best way to live. There is simple comfort to be found in being able to enjoy the moment, no matter what the moment, and finding something happy. It is all about simplicity—it is about being able to enjoy yourself and find happiness wherever you can find it.

Perhaps the most important takeaway point for you about the hygge lifestyle is that you simply want to enjoy the moment. You need to let go of the fears and uncertainties that may otherwise plague you. Live a little. Enjoy that drink. Go out with your friends. Eat that second serving of pasta that you probably do not need but really want to enjoy. It can help you begin to eliminate the stress that you feel, slowly letting it go and basking in a comfortable, contented life, free from the grip of stress.

**Yoga Lifestyle**

Yoga is so much more than just poses and breathing. It is not just being able to become flexible or learn how can change the ways that you move. It is about developing a new worldview; it is a philosophy that brings together the body and mind. It is a way to live your life, free from the entrapments of stress that can drag you down. It is to look at the lifestyle in hopes of bringing balance to yourself, not just physically, but mentally as well. It is to find that perfect balancing act between how you stand and how you hold your mind. It is the ability to be able to better manage yourself. It is to be able to adopt the principles that will keep you healthy, of body and mind. It is to live; it is to dedicate yourself wholly and utterly to the principles of yoga. It is to be willing and able to allow yoga to become your entire life. You will live yoga. You will breathe yoga. You will let yoga guide each and everything that you do in your own life, and in doing so, you will discover something incredible: Peace of mind and harmony of self is something that you can, in fact, achieve.

The yoga lifestyle has several different aspects that come together. However, there is one catch: You must always give everything that you do, no matter what it is, your fullest, complete attention. You must make sure that you are always concentrating in the moment, focusing on what you are doing and making sure that you are living your best life for yourself. Recognize that you need to be able to spend that time focusing entirely on yourself. Pay attention to the fact that, at the end of the day, you *need* to work hard. You must make sure that you dedicate yourself to everything you do.

To live the yoga lifestyle, you must follow several important principles. Unlike hygge, yoga is a bit more structured in the lifestyle and the rules. While hygge focused on a feeling, these focus on the lifestyle entirely—you must remember the five yamas of yoga:

- You must be nonviolent—to yourself or others.

- You must be honest and truthful in everything that you say, and you must make sure that you always stop and consider what will happen if you say something, before you speak.

- You must ensure that you only take what you need at any point in time; do not be greedy and do not steal from others.

- You must remain committed to yourself, your relationships, and the lifestyle that you have chosen.

- You must live a life of minimalism.

Maintaining that is a powerful thing; it can help you immensely. It can help you discover what it is that you want to do and how you will do it. It will guide you toward the right attitude to retain your peace of mind. To live that life, you must make sure that your entire lifestyle follows the same principles. You must make sure that you:

- Eat healthily to ensure that your body, and therefore the mind as well, become healthy.

- Maintain control over yourself and pay attention to the ways in which you conduct yourself around other people.

- Meditate often and make it a daily habit.

- Relax and let go of the stressors that hold you back. Learn to let go of the negativity and embrace the moment.

- Think positively and make sure that you always resist the urge to fall into negative thinking.

- Breathe deeply and regularly; defeat the stressors before they can drag you down and hold you back. The more that you can breathe and the better that you can relax, the better you will do.

Remember, yoga is about living peacefully. It is about being at peace with yourself and making sure that your body is healthy. When your body is healthy, you can focus your mind on what matters. When your body and mind are healthy, only then can you begin to recognize that you need a calm heart to rely on greatly as well. If you can do so, you can live a life that will serve you well. It will guide you toward the peace that you are seeking and enable you to better achieve the peace that you need.

## CHAPTER 4: DELETING DAILY STRESS: PREPARING FOR RELAXATION

Now, at this point, you have gone over the vast majority of the important information. You have been guided through how to identify your stress. You have discovered how to remove the power from your stress. Now, it is time to prepare your environment. It is time for you to begin to recognize that everything that you do, your environment, and everything around you is all intertwined. It is time to remember that, ultimately, the stress that you feel can be left behind. It is time to see the ways in which you can begin to defeat it all. It is time for you to recognize the ways in which you can stop the stressors before they can get worse. It is time to learn how best you can guide your own life and begin to recognize the necessary changes that you need to make. If you can do that, little by little, you can begin to relax.

Within this chapter, it is a time for preparation. We are going to prepare your environment; you will be guided through everything that you will need to ensure that your environment is calming. Perhaps you are going to set up a place of meditation or yoga—that would be a great use of your time and space. Perhaps you are going to take a look at the ways in which you can change your own mind, little by little. Perhaps you need to stop and recognize the relaxation techniques that you will be introduced to shortly as we begin going into meditation and mindfulness practices.

As you go through this chapter, pay close attention to the environment that you are regularly in. Look at the ways in which your environment needs to change. See the ways that you may need to change up how you interact with the environment around you. Consider for a moment how your environment is working for you—and how it is holding you back at the same time. Consider the ways in which you can do better for yourself; recognize what you could change to allow yourself to relax as well. And finally, remember to keep an open mind as you go through this chapter. Recognize the changes that you can make and the significance to doing so.

**The Relaxing Environment**

Think about it for a moment—you have rooms for all sorts of purposes in your home. You have the living room, for entertainment. You have the kitchen, for cooking. You have the dining room, for eating. A bedroom is for sleeping and a bathroom is for bathing. However, none of that is necessarily calming or for relaxing. It is time for you to consider what you will need to ensure that you have a place that will cue to you that it is time to relax—it could be a small nook in your home. It could be a spot under a tree in your yard. It could be in your bedroom or somewhere else dedicated to you. No matter where it is, however, you need a spot that is dedicated—it should be a place in which you focus entirely on your relaxation. It is a place of quiet contemplation and meditation. It will be somewhere that you can softly retreat to when you feel your mind beginning to become overwhelmed in its current environment or setting.

This space should, ideally, serve as your meditation space as well. As you continue throughout this book, you will find that you are given several meditations to practice and as you practice them, you want to ensure that you are back to being able to relax with ease. You want to be able to ensure that, at the end of the day, you can focus, that you can unwind. You want to have a place that you associate solely with meditation—and this will be the place for you. There are no rules as to where it is or what it should be—but it should give you that sense of peace and purpose.

Your place of relaxation should be somewhere that you will feel calm within. It should be somewhere somewhat isolated, so you know that you will not be distracted by people running back and forth. Nothing is more distracting than trying to meditate in your back yard, only to have your children constantly running back and forth, shrieking with joy as they chase each other. You need somewhere that is peaceful to you and quiet. It should be somewhere that you can go and immediately feel calmer. Keep in mind that, while you can meditate anywhere, it is always better to find somewhere that you will be left to your own devices and peace.

The room should be clean and free from clutter—if you are in a closet, for example, the clutter will distract you. You want to have somewhere that you can look without really seeing anything; you want a clean floor, or clear, organized walls. It does not have to be perfectly blank, but the more cluttered that the environment that you have chosen is, the more likely you are to find that you cannot focus with the attention that you need.

Likewise, it should also be somewhere comfortable. You do not have to sit cross-legged if you do not want to—you are free to take any positions that you want to, so long as you are comfortable where you are. If you do have to sit on the floor, you may want to consider the use of something plush to sit on to ensure that you do not get uncomfortable. Remember, there are no rules that say that meditation needs to be uncomfortable. On the contrary, it should be something that you can really enjoy.

The lighting in your area should also be something calming. In particular, you may want to make use of natural light over anything else. You can use sunlight, or if you are meditating somewhere darker or at night, you can choose to use some candles if you prefer. Using natural light will always be preferred; it is less harsh and is more likely to help you begin to relax, little by little.

You may also want to consider bringing some plants into your area; remember, nature is incredibly relaxing on its own and it is not always possible to be able to meditate in peace outside. Sometimes, what you really need is to be able to look at a plant, growing peacefully in your meditative space if you can.

Some people find that they make use of aromas to help themselves calm down as well, but this one is very highly a personal preference. If you find that there are some scents that immediately help you to settle down, you may benefit from the use of incense or candles. It can help you focus mindfully on the moment, really exploring the scent as you focus on it. It can also help you to relax if you use some of the scents, such as lavender, that are inherently calming to us as a species. No matter the method that you prefer to use, however, one thing is for sure—you need to decide what works best for you. If you find that incense or candles give you migraines, you are likely better avoiding them entirely.

**Preparing for Relaxation**

When it comes to relaxing itself, it is very important that you aim to bring at least 30 minutes of relaxation to your life per day. This should be time that you can rely on yourself to relieve the tension. Remember, living a life of peacefulness is not easy. It is not effortless. Part of the effort that you will need to include in the process is ensuring that you are able to relax and that you implement it regularly to ensure that, at the end of the day, you are better able to focus. If you can do so, you will find that you are more relaxed in general. You will find that you will be able to enjoy yourself more than ever. All you have to do is make sure that you implement these changes to your life.

To begin, get into your nice and quiet place that you have set up according to the information that you have just received. It can be anywhere, so long as you are comfortable. Get into a good position for yourself—legs crossed or uncrossed depending upon what it is that you would prefer to be in. Enjoy the space and the sensations.

As you prepare to relax, ensure that you are not wearing anything that is restrictive; you want to be free to move however it is that you feel compelled to do so. You want to be free from your shoes, if you can be. Make sure that, for the duration of your relaxation or your meditation, you will not be interrupted. This means that you should set your phone to do not disturb mode or turn it off entirely. It should be put away somewhere that will not distract you at all. Make sure that, if your door locks and it is safe to do so, you lock it.

Close your eyes as you prepare to relax and notice the way that your body feels. Start at the top of your head and slowly work your way down, checking in with each and every part of your body to see how it is that you feel. You should do this slowly but surely; watch to see the ways in which your body changes as you eventually go through your meditation.

**Relaxation Breathing**

To be able to follow through with the meditations that you are about to be provided, you will need to do something in particular—you will need to allow yourself to breathe. It is time for you to learn how to properly breathe—though we all breathe on a daily basis, constantly inhaling and exhaling, a shocking majority of people do not actually breathe properly. A great deal of people breathe in ways that are not conducive to relaxation. They may breathe in ways that are actually contradictory—they may find that, at the end of the day, their breathing is actually heling to raise their anxiety levels rather than to allow them to be mitigated and slowed down. It is important to watch the ways that this plays out. It is crucial for you to stop and feel the ways in which your breathing changes your body.

Let's experiment with the ways that breathing can change up how you feel for a moment. Begin by taking a normal breath for a moment. Keep up those normal breaths for yourself. Breathe in and out naturally, without feeling the need to change them. Allow yourself to feel the ways that you breathe and allow yourself to focus on the sensation. How are you feeling right now? Do you feel tense? What do you notice about your heart?

Now, speed up your breathing. For the next minute, breathe rapidly, in and out, at double the speed, at least. Be careful not to hyperventilate here; we are not aiming for you to pass out—you simply want to feel how your body responds as your breathing continues to change as well. As you breathe quicker, you may notice that your chest tightens up a bit. You may feel a bit more energized and alert. You may feel that familiar sensation of anxiety building up as well.

Now, suddenly slow down your breathing. You want to take big, deep breaths here that fill up your lungs. Breathe in deeply to the count of five. Then, hold the breath in your lungs for a moment to allow the breath to slowly exit your body. You should be pacing your breathing to at just 6 breaths per minute, in and out, slowly breathing in and letting the air linger in your lungs. As you do this, pay careful attention to how you are breathing. To get the best effect, you should find that as you breathe, your stomach moves in and out further than your chest. This is how you know that you are making use of what is known as diaphragmatic breathing—this is the breathing that you are looking for when you move down toward the meditations.

Reflect on the way that these breaths have made you feel. You should find that you feel calmer now; that you feel more in control of yourself and more capable than ever to self-regulate. If that is the case, then rest assured; you have succeeded. Remember this breathing method, and any time that you find that you are feeling stressed out or out of control, you can make use of these methods. You can breathe in and out slowly and surely to allow yourself to begin to relax.

## CHAPTER 5: BEDTIME STORIES: MINDFUL IMAGINATION

Encouraging a child's imagination is one of the most rewarding things that we can do as parents, and when it develops alongside a thorough grounding in mindfulness, then it can flourish along with an appreciation of the present moment. Helping children attain a sense of mindfulness is a way in which to foster gratitude with all the little things in life, as well as cultivating an understanding of how to slow down, focus the mind, and use the senses in order to truly experience all that life has to offer. The results of encouraging mindfulness in children are many: practicing mindfulness leads to lower levels of stress and anxiety; it helps to prevent depression; it is linked to better performance in school, because of increased focus and cognitive ability; and it can help kids to manage their emotions in constructive ways. Practicing mindfulness, alongside meditation, is a powerful tool that parents can teach their children—a tool that is accessible anywhere the child travels in life.

There is also an undeniable benefit in making a designated effort to spend quality time with your children. It is not enough to hope that your children feel safe, secure, and loved; you must put time, energy, and resources into that project if you want to foster an anxiety-free, low-stress childhood. Making a habit of spending this kind of quality time with a child is important to their mental and social development. It also creates a child with an optimistic, positive attitude—a child that feels confident that someone will be there for them when things are difficult. Mindfulness is also all about the cultivation of self-regulation of learning how to cope with difficult emotions and difficult circumstances when they arise. It teaches us to view daily life with appreciation and not to take good things for granted. In fact, with the cultivation of mindfulness comes the ability to view difficulty through a different perspective: you are giving your children the tools to reframe events and feelings through a healthy lens. If we realize that this bad moment or this bad feeling is only one moment in time—it will pass—

then we are better able to handle negative thoughts and circumstances as they arise. This is a coping mechanism that will serve anyone well throughout their childhoods and into adulthood.

The following stories in this section are designed to promote a sense of basic mindfulness, based on the five senses: sight, sound, smell, taste, and touch. This is a fundamental way in which a young child can learn how to access the world; without the expansive vocabulary of the adult world, a child experiences the world, first and foremost, through their five senses. This is a way into the practice of mindfulness, from the personal out into the physical world. These stories are meant to be imaginative exercises, with the parent relaying the story to the child as the child imagines their senses engaged with various stimuli. It is up to the parent and child together (and dependent on the age of the child) how interactive the stories can be. They can also be instructive in teaching young children some basic concepts relating to the five senses. The stories in Part III are expressly designed for helping children drift off to sleep, though the stories here can also be used in that way. Mostly, these stories are designed to get a child to start thinking about how he or she interacts with the world through their very own senses. It may seem a simple thing because it very much is: embracing the simplicity of life, accepting what is as it is, and cultivating gratitude for daily gifts is at the heart of mindfulness practice.

There is no single correct way to introduce these stories to children, but if you are trying to teach children some basic concepts (say, they are still learning how to identify colors), then you might consider having some small props on hand. Having a basic visual aid might be useful, depending on the context. It is also recommended by most experts to have some sort of soothing music playing in the background as you read bedtime stories to children—especially if your main goal is to get them to drift calmly to sleep. Still, even without visual or aural aids, these stories will fulfill the basic purpose of fostering mindfulness and alleviating stress at the end of a long day. Some stories will have some bracketed, italicized instructions for parents to follow if desired. Ultimately, reading these stories to children can be just as therapeutic to parents as to the children themselves. You will find your own anxiety and stress decrease as you encourage your children to practice mindfulness while helping them get to sleep peacefully. The more peaceful the children, obviously, the more peaceful the parents.

As we navigate an increasingly technologically dominated world, returning to some basic principles of happiness, togetherness, and a sense of psychological well-being can help to ground children in feelings of comfort and security. Making a nightly habit of reading bedtime stories to your children can not only cultivate a deeper sense of mindfulness and gratitude but also foster a developing imagination and a lifelong love of reading—not to mention creating a special bond between you and your children. As discussed in the first chapter of the book, parents are role models for their children, and demonstrating the power of stories and of imagination as well as the soothing calmness of mindfulness will equip your children to navigate all of the winding roads of life. This habit can dispel anxiety, soothe stress, eliminate fears, and encourage children to anticipate an always positive tomorrow.

## CHAPTER 6: COLOR CONCENTRATION

[*When you are ready to begin the story, be sure that you and your child have found a comfortable space that will remain quiet and free of distraction for the duration of the story.*] Now, start to relax and get ready for the story: arrange your body in a comfortable position; lay down and relax or close your eyes. Just be certain that you find a comfortable position for you, one in which you can stay still and focused on yourself throughout the story.

Once you are in your comfortable position, start to relax your body and tune into your breath. Soften your gaze so that you are looking at nothing in particular, or close your eyes so that you can focus clearly on your breath and your body. Start to find your natural breathing pattern and keep it slow and steady, breathing in and out, a natural inhale, and a natural exhale. Just listen to your own rhythms and trust them to keep your breath flowing naturally, in and out, in tune with your body and mind.

Start to relax the body while your eyes are closed, or your gaze is softened, and your breath is naturally flowing in and out of you, in and out. Feel your face relax, with your forehead smooth, your eye sockets soft, and still, your jaw loose. Let your throat relax, and just continue to breathe in tune with your body. This is not the time for effort or exertion; you are just listening to the natural rhythms of your body, slowly relaxing your head and neck, moving down to your shoulders, releasing any tension there. Your arms should be relaxed, as well, while your hands are still and comfortable by your side or in your lap. All the while, you are focused on nothing but the natural rhythm of your breath as it fills you with calmness. Let your body relax all the way down through your whole entire body, letting go and allowing yourself to just be with your breath and your body. Let your legs relax against whatever surface you are on, and

release your ankles and feet from any tension there, too. You are breathing in and out, one with your body in a state of calm relaxation.

Now, let's think about the beautiful nature of colors. Think about your own favorite color for a minute. Whether it's blue or red or green or purple, think about how that color makes you feel. Think about why it's your favorite color. Why does it make you happy? Spend some time breathing and thinking about all the feelings you have when you focus on your favorite color.

Maybe your favorite color is red: red is a bright color, full of energy and life—just like you are! [*If your child is still learning colors, you might show an example of each of the colors as they come up in the script.*] Red reminds us of fire, of glowing embers in the coals, of heat and sunlight. We can think of pretty birds, with bright red feathers, flying through the sky and singing their happy songs. We can think of Superman's cape flowing behind him, a symbol of power and strength as he races through the sky to help save someone. Or, maybe we can think of Spiderman's costume, with its bright red and spider web designs. Spiderman's red is also a glow of strength and power, and one of his powers is to use his "spidey senses" to hear or feel things that other people miss. You can do that, too, when you let your mind relax when you try to notice everything around you. Think about that for a minute, while you keep your breath slow and steady: what do you notice right now? [*Depending on the goal here, you might encourage your child to listen for a minute and report on what he or she notices, or you might encourage them just to think about it silently.*]

Or, maybe your favorite color is yellow, like a big ball of sunshine and happiness bursting out of you. Yellow is bright and bold, and it makes your imagination glow. You can also think of shimmering showers of gold glitter, brightening the day for everyone around you, or a big pile of shiny gold coins left behind as treasure for some lucky kid to find. Or, you can think of the shiny yellow color of a rain jacket, making the day brighter and more fun for everyone during a gentle rain fall. Yellow is also the color of little baby ducks, all sweet and fuzzy and small, waddling their way into the pond with their cute little quacks. [*If you're still interested in interacting, you might have the child imitate the ducks.*] When you think of yellow, you are light and happy like a warm summer day when you get to play outside until it's time for dinner. Yellow makes you want to laugh at all the funny things in the world. While you keep breathing slowly in and out, think about how yellow makes you feel. [*Again, this can be time for some quiet reflection—or nodding off to sleep—or a moment for some open discussion.*]

Perhaps your favorite color is orange, a mix of fiery red and bright yellow. Orange glows with happiness and makes your day feel a little bit bolder. It is also warm like late afternoon sunshine, glowing with health and energy. It makes us feel awake and warns us of caution, like the big orange cones on the side of the road while men are working on it. An orange is also something good to eat, juicy and sweet, and sticky. It makes us feel adventurous and ready to make up a great story. It can also make us think of the fall and Halloween, carving up a big orange pumpkin to put out for trick-or-treaters. Orange is also the color of Thanksgiving, with its pumpkin pie and roasted turkeys and other bright treats. When the fall comes, the leaves on the trees slowly change from green to gold and orange and brown. Orange takes us from summer to fall into winter, slowly moving the seasons along. It brightens our mood and then calms us down. We watch the orange leaves drift and twist in the breeze.

Maybe your favorite color is green, like the biggest field of grass in the middle of summer or the tops of trees when everything is coming to life after winter. Maybe you like the bright green of moss on the tops of rocks or at the corners of ponds, while you think of exploring everything beautiful in nature around you. Green is the color of the jumping frogs and the darting lizards, funny creatures that live just outside our doors. It's the color of turtles, even famous turtles like the Teenage Mutant Ninja Turtles, with their big shells and funny actions. Green makes us think of life and growth, the stalks of flowers, and the leaves on trees, all reaching up from the earth to the sun. Green keeps us close to the earth, in harmony with nature. You can also think of the sparkly green of emerald stones or beautiful princess eyes. Or, you can think of other superheroes, with their shining green costumes, like the Green Lantern or the super-strong Hulk, whose very skin is green. What do you think of when you think of green? Could it be your favorite color? [*Another moment to pause, either for thought or dialogue.*]

Or, maybe your favorite color is purple, the color of magic and wizards, of fantasy and rainbows. It is a mysterious color, a mix of many colors to make a lot of different types of purple. Purple is a deep color, and you can see it almost anywhere, from purple shirts to bright purple flowers at the beginning of spring. Purple seems like such a magic color, but you can find it everywhere in nature, from flower to food. Purple is the color of grapes and grape juice, and there are even purple potatoes if you can believe it! Purple is also the color of the night sky when the evenings are warm, and the night comes creeping in. You can even smell the color purple when the flowers bloom in spring, and in the lavender that grows in the garden. There are also tiny purple fish in the sea that glow with energy and dart about among the seaweed.

Purple is also the color of kings, with their magnificent robes and great wealth. It is a strong, sturdy color, just like the people who love it best. Is purple your favorite color? Think about why purple makes you feel happy, while still remembering to breathe in and out, eyes closed and relaxed.

Maybe, though, your favorite color is blue, one of the best colors in the world. Blue is the color of our very planet, mostly, with its big wide oceans and lovely lakes covering so much of the surface. Imagine a big blue ball in the dark sky of space, glowing with life and motion. We live in the color blue all the time, under bright blue skies that make us want to run and play, or in glittering blue ice that keeps us inside and warm by the fireplace. Blue is the color of peace. It makes us feel calm and safe, wrapped up in the skies and sunlight. It is the color of water, flowing freely from place to place, bringing life to all the plants and animals of the world. We feel at home in blue, because it represents life and peacefulness. In the depths of the deep blue sea, we find all the most fascinating things in life and nature. Blue can also be the color of our favorite pair of jeans, making us cozy and comfortable. And a blue ribbon can make us feel special because we've won something for what we did.

Now, then, think about all the amazing colors you get to see every day. Notice them when you think about it, and look at them with interest and feeling. Colors are important to how we feel and how we think about things. Think about your favorite colors and why they are your favorites. Every color should have some happiness for you, and you should feel pleased that all of these colors are out there in the world for you to enjoy and embrace. Colors make the world a beautiful place, and all of the colors that we can imagine or create are beautiful in their own way, just as we are all beautiful in our own lucky ways.

Now, return to your breath again, slowly breathing in and out, in and out. Let your whole body relax, and think about tomorrow and all the colors it will have to offer. Start to imagine that all of your favorite colors are dancing around with each other, swirling in and out of each other, changing slightly and becoming lighter at moments, darker at others. Brighter, then lighter. Bolder, then darker. All of these colors start to fade in and out, in and out, just like the rhythm of your breath. They grow closer and closer together until they all blend together, into one, growing darker as your eyelids grow heavier. They start to slow down as they settle into each other, turning the brightness of the day into the soothing calm of night; the colors start to fade into the nighttime, turning purple with dusk then fading further still into the smooth black of night. They are ready and waiting for you to greet them again another day. The colors follow you slowly into sleep, making bright dreams for a beautiful tomorrow.

## CHAPTER 7: SOUNDING SURPRISE

*[Make sure everyone is ready for bed and tucked in before beginning the story, which moves from bold sounds to subtle sounds into silence, allowing the child to drift calmly into sleep. This is also a good place to provide some background music on which the child can focus as he or she drifts off to sleep. While this is often a good idea, in an exercise on sound, it is even more appropriate.]* Prepare yourself and your space for bedtime before you begin: turn off all lights and glowing devices; turn down your covers and arrange your sleeping area how you like. Slowly ease into a lying down position. However, it feels most comfortable to you: you can lay on your back with your arms soft by your sides or spread out like a star pattern; you can lay on your side in a

cozy fetal-style position; you can lay on your belly with your head cushioned on your arms. Whatever is most comfortable for you is what is best.

Once you have found your position, begin to focus on the breath: you are breathing inward to fill your whole body with air, with life, with calm; you are breathing outward to disgorge any tension, release any negativity, and relax into your position. Breathe in, feeling the sensation of your chest expanding, your lungs and belly filling with air. Imagine that the breath fills your entire body, pushing upward from the lungs into the heart, the throat, the head, and pushing downward from the lungs to reach your tummy, your legs, your feet. Take a few moments to find the steady and natural pace of your breath, making sure you are comfortable and relaxed.

Now, let's think about what we hear throughout the day and how special those sounds can be. What do you hear in the morning? It depends on the time of year, but for much of the year, we get to hear the lovely sounds of the birds chirping. Sometimes we become so familiar with sounds that we barely hear them anymore. Think about how the birds sound where you live. Do they all sound the same? Which ones do you like the best? *[Engage in some light interaction here, reminding the child to be mindful of daily sounds, thankful for their presence.*] You can also hear the sound of the wind outside. Sometimes it's a gentle breeze, making a soft "whooo-shing" sound; sometimes, it's a strong gust, making the skies sound like they are howling. The sound of the wind changes every day.

You can also hear the sound of the wind and the sound of nature in the trees. The rustling of the leaves in the breeze can be very comforting, very calming. It can also mean that there is some small animal in the tree, a bird building a nest, or a squirrel hiding his nuts. If you listen closely to nature, you can hear what's going on even if you cannot see it. There are also ways that we can create more sound with the wind, like wind chimes. Have you ever heard a wind chime? What did it sound like? How did that sound make you feel?

There are also different sounds as the weather changes. In spring, you might hear the sounds of gentle rain streaming outside your window, or the loud sounds of a thunderstorm gathering clouds. The gentle rain is soothing and calming, as it brings water to the newly forming flowers and baby animals. You can also hear the sound of birds bathing in the newly fallen rain, splashing about in puddles, cleaning their feathers. In summer, you might hear the funny chirp of crickets playing outside, or sometimes when one wanders inside, you can hear him all the time! The buzzing of a fly in the window might annoy you, but it's another sound that makes you notice all the nature around you, even if you live in the middle of a city. You might also hear the sounds of lawnmowers growling outside, making the yards neat and clean, or the sounds of water sprinklers keeping the grass green and helping gardens to grow. You might also hear the sounds of other kids splashing through the sprinklers or laughing in backyard pools, playing, and having fun. In fall, you might hear the breeze blow through the trees and the soft rustling of leaves. If you listen hard enough, you might even hear the leaves falling, slowly whirling, down to the ground. You can hear the crunch of leaves underfoot when people walk up and down the sidewalks, and every once in a while, you might hear a gentle plop! when an acorn falls to the ground. In winter, you might hear the howling winds of a snowstorm or the icy sound of sleet. If you're lucky, depending on where you live, you might hear the soft sound of snow falling, and the whooshing of boots walking through the freshly falling snow. Maybe you'll hear the scrape of a snow shovel clearing a walkway or a sled gliding down a hill with kids laughing and playing.

Take a few minutes to think about what your favorite sounds might be: it can be anything you want it to be, from the sound of your best friend's laugh to the special effects in your favorite movie. Maybe it's the way your cat purrs when you rub his ears just right, or how your dog makes soft barking noises when you play fetch with her. Maybe you like the sound of your bike soaring along the sidewalk or over gravel, picking up speed as you go, or perhaps it's the sound of a car engine revving up ready to go. Maybe you like the sounds of sports, the crack of a ball against a bat, or the way a football thuds into someone's arms or the satisfying swack of a tennis ball against a racket. Perhaps you like the sounds of fans yelling support for their teams or the way that an audience claps when you have performed well. You might simply like the sound of someone's voice, your mom or dad or sister or brother or best friend when they talk to you about something fun. We all have sounds that make us feel happy and energized, or content and soothed. The sound of a pot boiling potatoes for your favorite dinner, or the timer in the kitchen going off as the roast is ready can remind us of all the things we love about our home.

There are lots of other human-made sounds, as well, beyond your personal space. Think about some of the other sounds you hear during the day: the noise of cars pulling into driveways or breezing by on highways, or the sound of tires crunching over gravel. Sometimes a distant honk sounds, punching through the quietness of the day. If you live in a small community, you might hear the sound of the noon bell, telling everybody what time it is. If you live in a big city, you might hear the sounds of lots of traffic, honking and braking, parking and going.  You might also hear the faraway sound of a plane from time to time, speeding through the air above you with a faint roar of the engine that is so very high up in the sky.  There might also be the sound of construction workers building things or repairing things, with their tools and ladders and helmets, the muffled conversation that you can't really hear the words to.  You can hear the sounds of electricity everywhere, if you listen hard enough, the calm buzz that hums away underneath all the other human sounds that we make every day.

Now, think about the sounds you hear when you are in school during the day.  There's the sound of the teacher's voice, which is hopefully a pleasant sound to you! And the sound of the markers squeaking against the board or the clack of fingers against a keyboard.  You might hear your fellow students murmuring to each other or chuckling under their breath.  You might hear the sound of a pencil or a crayon on paper, finishing a task, or imagining a drawing.  From time to time, you might hear someone in the back coughing or clearing their throat, small sounds that fill in our ears without us really noticing.  That's the special thing about noticing; you become more aware of everything around you and whether it's important to you.  You develop a better set of senses when you pay attention.

Remember not to forget where you are right now, breathing slowly in and out, in and out. What do you hear right now? The sound of your mom or dad reading to you, of course, but what else? You might hear some soft music that is playing in the background, helping you to relax and be calm. Think about the music, and how it makes you feel all calm and comforted. Be quiet for a minute and notice what else you hear around you. [*Encourage the child to be still and quiet, just breathing, and let them just think about what they hear; this should start to ease them into a state of relaxation headed toward sleep.*] You might also hear the quiet hum of the heater during colder months or the air conditioner if it's warmer. You might hear the faint sounds of your siblings or other family members in the house, getting ready to go to bed just like you. Their voices are soothing comforts, knowing that there are lots of loved ones surrounding you. You might hear the distant sounds of traffic outside or of neighbors visiting on the porch or in the courtyard. Listen to the sounds of the weather, too: is it quiet and still, or rainy and gloomy; do the trees rustle, or are they quiet tonight? Can you hear any animals, scurrying about at night, looking for food and a warm place to sleep? Are there any dogs barking or cats meowing? All of these everyday sounds fill us with familiar comfort, as we know that they were there yesterday and they will be there tomorrow, too.

Think about the sounds of your bedroom, too, the creak of a floorboard or the soft closing of the door. Your bed makes a soft sound like sighing when you sink into it, with your head heavy and ready for sleep. The sheets rustle softly against your skin, and you might hear yourself yawn as you slowly drift into sleep. Pull the blanket up around you and snuggle in as you start to let go of all this hearing, falling down into sleepy time. This is the biggest surprise of all, the sound that silence makes when you start to fall deep into the rhythms of sleep. You are aware of the sounds around you, but you are letting those go in favor of listening to the calming sound of your own mind falling to sleep. There are beauty and comfort in that quietness, like drifting away on a puffy cloud that moves gently across the horizon. There is no breeze to disturb you, no rustling of trees, just the small quietness of your mind drifting off to dreams. You can no longer hear the sound of yourself breathing, you are just aware of the gentle rise and fall of your chest, as you enter into the safe space of dreams.

As you have noticed all these sounds, think about how comforting they are, how familiar and safe and secure. Start to let your eyes and ears close, letting the sounds and thoughts drift away. Now that you can notice the silence, calm, and close around you, you can let go of the day and of all that you see and hear, sinking slowly into sleep. Breathe deeply and hear the sound of calm silence as you fall gently asleep, ready again to hear all the world has to offer again tomorrow.

## CHAPTER 8: SMELL-O-VISION

[*When you are ready to begin the story, be sure that you and your child have found a comfortable space that will remain quiet and free of distraction for the duration of the story. This can be in bed or in a traditional meditative position.*] Now, start to relax and get ready for the story: arrange your body in a comfortable position, lay down and relax or close your eyes. Just be certain that you find a comfortable position for you, one in which you can stay still and focused on yourself throughout the story.

Once you are in your comfortable position, start to relax your body and tune into your breath. Soften your gaze so that you are looking at nothing in particular, or close your eyes so that you can focus clearly on your breath and your body. Start to find your natural breathing pattern and keep it slow and steady, breathing in and out, a natural inhale, and a natural exhale. Just listen to your own rhythms and trust them to keep your breath flowing naturally, in and out, in tune with your body and mind.

Start to relax the body while your eyes are closed, or your gaze is softened, and your breath is naturally flowing in and out of you, in and out. Feel your face relax, with your forehead smooth, your eye sockets soft, and still, your jaw loose. Let your throat relax, and just continue to breathe in tune with your body. This is not the time for effort or exertion; you are just listening to the natural rhythms of your body, slowly relaxing your head and neck, moving down to your shoulders, releasing any tension there. Your arms should be relaxed, as well, while your hands are still and comfortable by your side or in your lap. All the while, you are focused on nothing but the natural rhythm of your breath as it feels you with calmness. Let your body relax all the way down through your whole entire body, letting go and allowing yourself to just be with your breath and your body. Let your legs relax against whatever surface you are on, and

release your ankles and feet from any tension there, too. You are breathing in and out, one with your body in a state of calm relaxation.

Now, let's start thinking about the power of smell: it's one of those senses that is with you all the time and in every way. Many people say that the sense of smell is the sense that is most associated with our memories, so we can think of many happy memories that certain smells remind us of. You probably have some personal memories about certain kinds of smells from your life. Take a few minutes to think about those smells and remember where you were and what you were doing. Breathe in slowly, remembering that certain smell, and exhale slowly, sinking into the happiness of the memory. [*Here, encourage your child to express some particular memories of particular events that are associated with smell. This promotes mindfulness of experience, as well as increases gratitude for past events and people.*]

Let's imagine some particular smells that are associated with particular things that we get to experience every day at certain times. The smell of the outdoors in springtime is one of the most marvelous smells we can imagine, wouldn't you think? It is the smell of newly cut grass and the buds on trees and the newly blossoming flowers you find in gardens all around. Breathing in and out, imagine a beautiful spring day and what you might smell when you get to go outside to play. Even the warming sunshine has its own fresh, clean smell, just like the fresh, clean smells of nature coming back to life after a long winter. You might also think about how it smells after a gentle spring rain, with everything washed clean and clear. After a rain, you will often hear the sounds of birds chirping and insects buzzing, as all the little creatures come out to get a drink of fresh rainwater. Slowing inhaling, think of that fresh rain smell, how clean it is as the sun peeks out again from the horizon. Slowly exhaling, think of how you feel when this spring rain is over, and you get to go back outside to play.

There are other smells in nature that are particular to certain places at certain times. If you have ever been to the mountains, you know that there are certain very mountain-y smells that you will encounter. Envision a mountain capped with snow and carpeted with trees, harboring lots of animals, from squirrels to deer. How does the mountain snow smell? It smells like cold and ice, like the sky, and the clouds have brought a fresh blanket to cover the land. The mountains often smell of pine trees, too, that clear, sharp scent that reminds you that the trees are living beings, breathing in and out, slowly and steadily, just as we do. If there is water nearby, and there are always streams or small lakes on a mountain, then you might smell the deep smell of moss and water, of frogs and fish. If you like to fish, then you know the smell of the lake or the pond and how clean the smell of fresh fish is. These deep smells remind us of how we are all, together, connected to each other and to nature. Breathe in and out, slowly and steadily, imagining how this mountain looks and sounds and smells. [*Take a few moments here to let your child's imagination roam. These brief intervals will also be signals for them to fall gently asleep if they are ready.*]

If you have not been to the mountains or if they are not your favorite spot, then another particular smell in nature that might be better for you is that of the beach and the ocean. This scene is another place that is rife with particular sights and sounds and smells. Think about how the sand smells when you play along the shoreline, running about collecting shells or building a magnificent sandcastle. It smells wet and deep, clinging to the mists of the ocean while also picking up the scents of the shore. Think about how the ocean smells, it salty spray washing up with the tide, crashing into the shoreline. The ocean smells of salt and minerals, filled with living things from the tiniest krill to the largest living animal on earth, the blue whale. There are also many, many plants in the sea, as well, so you can imagine the smell of kelp forests or floating groups of algae, with briny and funky scents.

There are large coral reefs to be found in the ocean, as well, with their bright colors and brighter fish darting in and out of these huge structures. Think of all of those magnificent things as you breathe in and out, slowly and steadily, imagining all of the glorious things that go into making up the scent of an ocean.

You can also think about a great campfire out on the lakeside or up on the beach, with the sounds of fire crackling as it cools down for the evening. The smell of the fire, burning wood, and embers are earthy and comfy, calling you in to sit by the fire to warm your hands when it starts to get cooler. You can also imagine the smells of food cooking, of hamburgers grilling and hot dogs searing on the hot grill. It makes your mouth water just thinking about these wonderful smells. You can also imagine that these smells are associated with celebrations, maybe the setting off of fireworks, which send off their own exciting smells of sparks and imitation smoke. Imagine the smells of these wonderful times of the year when you are hanging out with family and friends in the summertime, happy and comfy and tired from the day's play. Take a few moments here to breathe in and out, slowly and steadily, while you remember those special times.

There are also numerous smells that remind us of the comforts of home, of course. Indeed, many of our favorite smells come out of our own memories of our favorite places to be. Think about the scent of fresh baking bread, coming out of the oven like the biggest hug from your favorite person. Or, think about the smell of bread toasting, if freshly baked bread isn't a familiar scent: the soft, sweet bread takes on the smell almost of fire, growing crunchy and charred with the heat. It's a very nice smell that makes you think of weekend mornings and cozy days. Think of the smell of sausages sizzling in the pan on the stovetop, or the scent of fresh juice being poured into a cup. This morning routine is comforting and wonderful. Take a few minutes to remember how all these smells make you feel. Breathing in and out, slowly and steadily, think of how these smells remind you of something happy.

You can also think about one of the happiest smells of childhood, the scent of cookies baking in the oven. You've helped your mom or dad, or grandma or grandpa, make this big batch of chocolate chip cookies. Think of the smell of the sugar and butter mixing together, how sweet it smells, combined with the deep cocoa smell of chocolate. That's what makes chocolate chip cookies so good, these different smells that grow out of the special magic between the sugar, eggs, and butter, and the yummy chocolate. Imagine how the cookies smell while they are in the oven, baking away. The whole house fills with this special scent, the cookies turning brown and spreading out on the sheet. This smell of sugar and chocolate baking makes for one of the best memories we can have. Imagine how happy it makes you to walk in the door after someone has been baking cookies. This is a happy place that you want to come back to all the time. Take a few minutes here to imagine this happy house with its comforting smells. [*Again, continue to allow them a little quiet time for their own imagination and dropping into gentle sleep.*]

Now, you can also think about the everyday smells of your own house, which is probably a little bit different from everyone else's. These are the smells that make you the most comfortable and warm, feeling loved and hugged all the time. It might be the smell of mom's perfume or dad's cologne that reminds you of home, or it might be the smell of fresh laundry coming out of the dryer, so wonderful when you crawl into a blanket that's still warm. It might be the smell of a favorite pet, who comes running to you with a cold nose and eager eyes, or who comes to sit in your lap quietly purring. These smells make us feel happy and loved. It might be the smell of cooking, your favorite roast or chicken dish or big pot of soup. The smell of a sizzling grilled cheese sandwich with a big bowl of tomato soup or a pan of macaroni-n-cheese: all of these food smells have a special place in your home. It could be what your bedroom smells like, a whole host of smells that only you understand in a special way.  The way your bed smells or your blanket or a favorite stuffed animal: imagine these smells, breathing slowly and steadily, and imagine that they hold you in loving arms, as you slowly fall to sleep, dreaming of all of the wonderful scents that you will get to smell tomorrow and the next day and the next.  Breathe in and out, in and out, knowing that with each breathe you smell love.

## CHAPTER 9: TASTING TREATS

[*When you are ready to begin the story, be sure that you and your child have found a comfortable space that will remain quiet and free of distraction for the duration of the story. Also, be aware that, since this story/meditation focuses on food, it might trigger a hunger response in the child. Be sure that he or she has a healthy treat before embarking on this one.*] Now, start to relax and get ready for the story: arrange your body in a comfortable position; lay down and relax or close your eyes. Just be certain that you find a comfortable position for you, one in which you can stay still and focused on yourself throughout the story.

Once you are in your comfortable position, start to relax your body and tune into your breath. Soften your gaze so that you are looking at nothing in particular, or close your eyes so that you can focus clearly on your breath and your body. Start to find your natural breathing pattern and keep it slow and steady, breathing in and out, a natural inhale, and a natural exhale. Just listen to your own rhythms and trust them to keep your breath flowing naturally, in and out, in tune with your body and mind.

Start to relax the body while your eyes are closed, or your gaze is softened, and your breath is naturally flowing in and out of you, in and out. Feel your face relax, with your forehead smooth, your eye sockets soft, and still, your jaw loose. Let your throat relax, and just continue to breathe in tune with your body. This is not the time for effort or exertion; you are just listening to the natural rhythms of your body, slowly relaxing your head and neck, moving down to your shoulders, releasing any tension there. Your arms should be relaxed, as well, while your hands are still and comfortable by your side or in your lap. All the while, you are focused on nothing but the natural rhythm of your breath as it feels you with calmness. Let your body relax all the way down through your whole entire body, letting go and allowing yourself to just be with your breath and your body. Let your legs relax against whatever surface you are on, and

release your ankles and feet from any tension there, too. You are breathing in and out, one with your body in a state of calm relaxation.

One of the most important senses in our lives is the sense of taste: it's an amazing ability to be able to taste all the treats that the world has to offer.  But, oftentimes, we eat without really thinking, taste without knowing why we like what we like.  The idea of spending some time thinking about tastes and how they make you feel certain ways is part of what happens when we practice mindfulness.  So, let's take some time and think about some of our favorite tastes and how they make us feel, making sure to keep your breath slow and steady, staying in tune with your mind and body. [*Give them a few minutes to talk or think about their favorite things to taste, allowing them the chance to contribute and to relax into the experience.*]

Now, let's think about a kind of daily routine that many of us share, with tastes that are similar to many of us living in a particular place in this particular time.  When we get up in the morning, we have to eat breakfast, sometimes boasted as the most important meal of the day.  It gives us the energy to think and play and go about our busy days.  So, what do you typically eat for breakfast?  Think about how that tastes, and what your favorite part of it is.  You might have some toast, hot and crunchy from the toaster, smeared with some butter or some jam or even some bright green avocado. Think about how a nice, hot piece of toast tastes, all crunch, then softness with the sweet and clean taste of bread. Maybe your bread is smooth and white, or maybe it is brown with some texture. Whatever kind you like, think of how it's taste and texture wake you up in the morning. Imagine that you're having some crisp bacon or some fresh sausage with your toast; think about the smells of cooking that get your mouth watering and ready for food. Imagine how good it feels to taste this delicious food and how it warms your body and gives you energy. Imagine that you're having a bit of juice or a piece of fruit with your breakfast; maybe instead of toast, you're having this with a big warm bowl of oatmeal. It tastes like comfort and warmth, the nutty taste of oatmeal mixed with the fresh tang of fruit. Imagine what your favorite warm breakfast is, breathing in and out, slowly and steadily, thinking about how these foods make you happy and strong.

Or, maybe you have a quick cereal breakfast some mornings or as a treat on weekends. This time, there is pleasure in the sugary taste and crunch of the cereal combined with the sweet taste of milk. Think about what cereal you like best and how best you like to eat it. There are cheerios with their toasty, nutty taste; topped with sliced bananas or strawberries, they are tangy and sweet, as well. There are rice chex with their clean, malty flavors and extra crunchy snap. There are all sorts of sugary cereals that you may get as a special treat, maybe with marshmallows or raisins or bright, brilliant colors. Notice that taste is as much about what we see and hear as what we actually taste: these bright colors might prepare you to expect a nice, sugary bite, while the crunch of the cereal against the smoothness of the milk feels really nice in your mouth. Think about the simple happiness that you can get from just a humble bowl of cereal.

Now, you have moved on to your daily activities, school at some times of the year, play at others. You have spent lots of energy after your breakfast, and now you are hungry for a nice lunch. This comes in many, many forms, so think about your very favorite lunch food. It could be something classic and simple, like a gooey grilled cheese with its buttery outside crunch and tangy, cheesy center. Even better, your sandwich comes with a steaming hot bowl of tomato soup, which you can dunk your sandwich in, contrasting the richness of the cheese with the tanginess of the soup. Or, maybe you like a peanut butter and jelly sandwich, all soft white bread and nutty, sweet flavors. Think about the pleasant squish of a peanut butter and jelly sandwich in your mouth and how those flavors go together so well. There are many other choices for lunch, as well, from cold cuts and chips to salads and soups and anything in between. Imagine your favorite lunchtime meal, remembering how it tastes and smells, thinking about how it makes you feel. [*Give them a minute of quiet breathing to think to themselves, which also starts to ease them into sleep.*]

Don't forget about particular foods, as well. The more we think about what we eat, enjoying each and every bite, the happier we are with what we have. Let's think about the simple joys of your basic apple. Not only does the old saying, "an apple a day keeps the doctor away," have some truth to it because apples are a healthy treat, but also does the apple satisfy the need for a quick snack. Imagine the apple, bright red or yellow-flecked or green, in your hand, shiny and beautiful with its bright colors. Think about the satisfying crunch when you take your first bite, and the sweet juice that runs into your mouth. An apple is really a complex flavor when you think about it, crunchy but smooth with sweetness at first followed by a little bit of tang. A regular old red apple can be just as juicy and sweet as anything, but a tart little green apple really has some bite. Think about what your favorite is, imagining how satisfying it is to crunch that sweet juiciness up. [*Obviously, use any healthful food here that your child likes, like carrot sticks or a different fruit if he or she doesn't enjoy apples.*]

Now, we come to what many people feel is the best meal of the day: dinnertime. Dinner wraps up our day with a final meal to give us the energy to get through the rest of our day, with homework or some fun downtime, as well as through the night while we sleep. Think about what you like your parents to make for your very favorite meal, the one you ask for on your birthday or other special occasions. This might be pizza with lots of gooey cheese and salty pepperoni, or macaroni and cheese with its soft, rich tanginess, or a big juicy hamburger, all beefy and strong, with a side of extra crispy French fries. Or, it could be your mom's or dad's best fancy dish, like a big pan of baked pasta with a tangy tomato sauce, lots of sharp cheese, and soft noodles. Or, this might be a big dish of pot roast with lots of soft, sweet vegetables in it like potatoes and carrots. Imagine your favorite dinnertime dish and how it fills you with comfort and love. Take a few minutes here to think about how everything tastes and how happy it makes you feel.

Now, we shouldn't forget about the dessert: if you are like most kids, you love some sweet stuff on occasion. You might enjoy a yummy piece of chocolate cake, deep with cocoa flavor, and the richness of sugary icing on top. Or, what about a chocolate chip cookie with crisp edges and a warm and gooey center? How about a chilly bowl of ice cream, flavored with chips or cookies, nuts, or caramel? Think about your favorite dessert and how special it is to be eating it: these tastes are really big tastes and, when you get to enjoy them, you should really take the time to think about how wonderful these tastes are and how they make you feel. Taking the time to taste everything fully means that we can really enjoy these treats when we get them.

But, of course, these kinds of sugary treats aren't the only kind of treats that make us happy. A single sweet apple or a handful of baby carrots dipped in ranch dressing or a nice piece of chicken with some buttery peas: the healthy stuff makes us happy, too. This kind of eating makes you feel better and sleep more soundly, giving your body all of the best things it needs to help you feel energetic and smart and cheerful every day.

Now, as you drift off to sleep, think about all of the wonderful tastes you get to experience each and every day. Think about how lucky you are to get to try all of these things, and remember that, even if you don't like something right away, you should try it again, just to see. Our sense of taste is a wonderful sense, bringing us pleasure and health all of the time. When we use it with a sense of mindfulness and gratitude, we can increase that pleasure with every bite. As you breathe in and out, slowly and steadily, think about all the thanks you have for all the foods you get to eat. Imagine your favorite treats and how special they are. Focusing on your breath, remember how these wonderful things make you feel, warm and happy and whole. You drift off to sleep, ready for all of tomorrow's terrific tastes.

# CHAPTER 10: TOUCHING TEXTURES

*[When you are ready to begin the story, be sure that you and your child have found a comfortable space that will remain quiet and free of distraction for the duration of the story. As this story deals with the sense of touch, you might want to have some sample objects for the child to feel. Have them maintain their relaxed state, with eyes closed, so they can simply experience the sense of touch.]* Now, start to relax and get ready for the story: arrange your body in a comfortable position; lay down and relax or close your eyes. Just be certain that you find a comfortable position for you, one in which you can stay still and focused on yourself throughout the story.

Once you are in your comfortable position, start to relax your body and tune into your breath. Soften your gaze so that you are looking at nothing in particular, or close your eyes so that you can focus clearly on your breath and your body. Start to find your natural breathing pattern and keep it slow and steady, breathing in and out, a natural inhale, and a natural exhale. Just listen to your own rhythms and trust them to keep your breath flowing naturally, in and out, in tune with your body and mind.

Start to relax the body while your eyes are closed, or your gaze is softened, and your breath is naturally flowing in and out of you, in and out. Feel your face relax, with your forehead smooth, your eye sockets soft, and still, your jaw loose. Let your throat relax, and just continue to breathe in tune with your body. This is not the time for effort or exertion; you are just listening to the natural rhythms of your body, slowly relaxing your head and neck, moving down to your shoulders, releasing any tension there. Your arms should be relaxed, as well, while your hands are still and comfortable by your side or in your lap. All the while, you are focused on nothing but the natural rhythm of your breath as it feels you with calmness. Let your body relax all the way down through your whole entire body, letting go and allowing yourself to just be with your breath and your body. Let your legs relax against whatever surface you are on, and

release your ankles and feet from any tension there, too. You are breathing in and out, one with your body in a state of calm relaxation.

Now, as we drift off to sleep, tonight, let's think about all the different textures in the world that we get to touch: smooth and rough, soft and hard, coarse and fine, and everything in between. Along with the senses of sight and sound and smell and taste, the sense of touch connects us to the world in many, many ways.

First, let's consider the texture of *smooth*, which is pleasing and quiet and can remind us of many things. Think of what a small pebble feels like in your hand, the kind with no edges or cracks, just a small round pebble that the water has washed to a smooth surface. It feels cool to the touch and familiar in the hand. It is not difficult or sharp, but so smooth you can feel it roll down your arm into the palm of your hand like a comforting gesture. Or, think of what a smooth surface is like, the top of a polished counter made of polished marble or granite. Or, perhaps the smooth silkiness of a satin shirt which rests against your body like a second skin. Or, perhaps the cool, smooth surface of a closed window, where your hand reaches for the outdoors but is stopped by the smooth, clear surface. How do you feel when you touch something smooth and silky, even and regular?

These kinds of textures can be very soothing and calming, with all their roughness smoothed away. Take some deep breaths here, thinking about how soothing it is to feel these even surfaces.

Now, let's think of the opposite: what is it like to touch something rough and bumpy, or sharp and prickly? If you think of the smooth rock above, now think of a rock that still has edges and cracks, or crystals and spikes. This rock may not be soothing, but it is powerful, with its mineral might on clear display. Touching this reminds you of the power of the earth to make these rocks and the power of weather to shape them into various forms. You may think of the wide variety of objects that nature creates over vast stretches of time. Or, you may imagine the way a regular leaf feels—all smooth and soft, with a bit of a rough stem—versus the way a pine needle feels, all sharp and hard. These things are both beautiful in their own way, the leaf a reminder of the lives that trees live with each cycle of the seasons, and the pine needle a reminder of how strong these particular trees are to live on through harsh winters. Think of the different ways that these different objects make you feel, while you remember to breathe in and out, slowly and steadily, staying in tune with your body as it gets heavier and sleepier.

There are all sorts of rough and interesting textures out there, some of them we are so used to touching that we don't even think about it. Think of how the strap on your book bag or backpack feels, with its slightly bumpy texture with its smooth fabric. Think of how the cover of a book feels, either hard and slick with laminated plastic or soft and pliable, moving easily beneath your fingertips. Think of how a screen feels to the touch, cold and satin-smooth, ready for the finger to move it this way and that. Imagine all of the wide variety of things that you touch when you go about your everyday routine. They come in all shapes, sizes, and they feel lots of different ways. While you breathe in and out, slowly and steadily, imagine in your mind the very many objects that you touch each and every day. [*Give them a few moments here to catalog their day, either verbally or silently. This might just encourage them to think their way into sleep.*]

When we think about texture, we don't always just think about how it feels when we touch it with our hands, but we also sometimes think about how something looks. If you think about how a solid color looks—let's say a solid blue t-shirt, for example—then we would say that it looks smooth or soft. But when you think about how a patterned set of colors looks—let's say a pair of plaid pants—then we would say that it looks bumpy or textured. The difference between a wall that is made up of one solid color versus a wall that is painted with designs gives us a sense that we experience the idea of texture through our eyes as well as through our hands. This is a really cool idea, because it shows us that all of our senses work together in different ways, and the way we experience the world is the result of our senses—sight, sound, smell, taste, and touch—giving us all sorts of information.

What about something that is grainy in texture, either fine or coarse depending on what it is? Think about how the sand feels when it runs through your hands or when you play with it on a beach. In the first case, the sand runs through your fingers, fine and smooth but not quite as smooth as silk; these are tiny grains, and you can feel the little bitty bumps as you let them run through your fingers. It is light and airy and makes a great soft landing should you need one. In the second case, when you build a sandcastle on the beach, the sand is coarser and wetter, almost like cement, so you can pack it together with your hands to make something that is almost solid but not quite. Sand is a magical substance, like water, that has the power to provide many different textures at once. Think about what kind of sand you like best and why. [*Pause here to let them think about it and relax into the sensation.*]

Speaking of water, this is one of the substances on earth that we touch all the time without even really thinking about it:

our bodies touch it when we take a bath or a shower; our tongues touch and taste it when we take a drink; and water can take on many, many different textures and forms. It is a liquid, smooth, and warm or cold and bracing. It is a solid in the form of ice, from the cubes we put into a drink to the surface that freezes over the top of a lake in winter. It is almost solid in the form of sleet and slush or snow and snowflakes. It is a gas, from the mist that forms in the early morning as fog to the evaporation that rises from a pot on the stove. Water transforms its textures into all kinds of pleasing and familiar things. The next time you come into contact with water, think about how it feels to the touch or to the taste. You will start to be amazed at how wonderful water really is.

You can also think about one of the best textures in the world, at least according to many people, that of soft and fluffy. This is one of the most soothing, calming, and happy-making textures that we run into during our daily lives. Think about petting your favorite animal, a pet, or something else you love: the soft, fluffy fur on a kitten or a puppy is one of the most pleasing textures in all of the world. Imagine how your pet feels, whether it be a dog or a cat, a turtle, or a fish. The way that they feel under your hand is one of the ways in which you learn how to connect with them, to love them. Think about your favorite stuffed animal, with its furry surface that you like to hug tight to you. That fuzzy feeling helps you feel safe and calm and relaxed.

Now, think about putting on your favorite sweater, worn soft with wear, or a nice fuzzy hat that keeps you warm when you go outside. A pair of fuzzy mittens to go with it, and no matter how cold it is outside, we feel safe and warm and wrapped up tight. You can also start to think about the way our favorite soft and fluffy pajamas feel when we put them on at night; this is perhaps one of the sleepiest feelings in the world, reminding us of bedtime and stories and super sweet dreams. Think about the softness of your favorite blanket, whether it be super fluffy or super smooth, wrapping you up in its warmth and comfort; think about the softness of your pillow as you sink your head into at night, all cool and smooth. Your bed, too, is soft and welcoming as you lay down on it, and it is also smooth and cool from the feel of the sheets over it. Notice that these kinds of soft are very different, the softness of a blanket that we hug close to us is different from the softness of the pillow that we lay our heads on. Breathing in and out, slowly and steadily, feel how the softness of your bed, your blanket, your pillow, and anything else you have hugs you into a sleepy, sleepy state. You feel relaxed and calm, breathing into the softness of your bed, hugging the warmness of your blanket. You fall slowly asleep; all tucked in tight in your safe, soft, and warm bed.

## CONCLUSION

Thank you for taking the time to make it to the end of this book, and hopefully, you will continue to use these methods and these meditations in your future. It is with the utmost sincerity that you are wished good luck in your endeavors. If this book has helped you with your goals at all, please consider heading over to Amazon to leave behind a review of just how much you have gotten out of this book; your opinions and your reviews are always greatly appreciated.